D1084952

MARTIAL ARTS
SPORTS ZONE

MIXED MARTIAL ARTS

ULTIMATE FIGHTING COMBINATIONS

Garrison Wells

Lerner Publications Company • Minneapolis

Lerner Publications Company
A division of Lerner Publishing Group, Inc.
241 First Avenue North
Minneapolis, MN 55401 U.S.A.

Website address: www.lernerbooks.com

Content Consultant: Greg Nelson, Brazilian jiujitsu black belt and mixed martial arts coach

Library of Congress Cataloging-in-Publication Data

Wells, Garrison.
    Mixed martial arts : ultimate fighting combinations / by Garrison Wells.
        p. cm. — (Martial arts sports zone)
    Includes index.
    ISBN 978-0-7613-8455-7 (lib. bdg. : alk. paper)
    1. Mixed martial arts—Juvenile literature. I. Title.
    GV1102.7.M59W45 2012
    796.815—dc23   2011038724

Manufactured in the United States of America
1 – BC – 12/31/11

Photo Credits: H. Rumph Jr./AP Images, 5; Jeff Chiu/AP Images, 6, 17, 26; Ryan Remiorz/AP Images, 7; Vladimir Korostyshevskiy/Shutterstock Images, 8; DEA/G. Nimatallah/De Agostini Picture Library/Getty Images, 9; Markus Boesch/Getty Images, 10; Holly Stein/Getty Images, 11; Sony Pictures Classics/Photofest, 13 (top); Lionsgate/Everett Collection, 13 (bottom); Kevin Lynch/Spike Television/Everett Collection, 14; Isaac Brekken/AP Images, 15; Eric Jamison/AP Images, 16, 24, 28 (top); Wally Santana/AP Images, 18; Ginger Monteleone/Bigstock, 19, 28 (bottom); Justin McKie/AP Images, 21; Felipe Dana/AP Images, 23; Nathan Denette/AP Images, 25; Neil Davidson/AP Images, 29
Backgrounds: Aleksandar Velasevic/iStockphoto, Tony Mathews/Fotolia
Cover: AP Photo/Eric Jamison (main); © iStockphoto.com/Aleksandar Velasevic (background).

Main body text set in ITC Serif Gothic Std Bold 11/17.
Typeface provided by Adobe Systems.

TABLE OF CONTENTS

CHAPTER ONE

OVERVIEW OF MIXED MARTIAL ARTS

During a light heavyweight match in 2009, mixed martial arts (MMA) fighter Anderson Silva defeated fighter Forrest Griffin. It only took three minutes and 23 seconds. Griffin was a bigger and heavier fighter than Silva was used to fighting. But Silva wanted a challenge. So he gained weight to be heavy enough to fight Griffin.

Silva planted a solid left hook on Griffin's face during the fight. The punch brought Griffin to the mat for the first time. Silva continued to pound Griffin while he was down. Silva then backed off so Griffin could stand up. But Griffin was drained. He fell into Silva's final punch. Griffin was out cold before hitting the ground.

Silva grew up in Brazil training in several martial arts styles. He learned Brazilian jiujitsu (a grappling, or ground-based, martial art) by watching other kids practice. He took lessons in tae kwon do (a Korean kicking martial art). Then he moved on to study Muay Thai (Thai boxing). In 2002 he started competing professionally in MMA. By mid-2006, Silva was fighting in the Ultimate Fighting Championship (UFC). He won Fight of the Year at the 2010 World MMA Awards for his fight against Chael Sonnen in UFC 117.

"I want to fight against the best. Whoever the best is at the time, that's who I want to fight."
—Anderson Silva

WHAT IS MMA?

MMA is a full-contact combat sport. Fighters showcase their skills and try to beat their competition. A match consists of two fighters going against each other in a caged ring.

MMA is a melting pot of martial arts and fighting styles. Its best fighters become stars. Besides Muay Thai and Brazilian jiujitsu, the sport features kickboxing, judo (a Japanese martial art), wrestling, and boxing. Fighters also use karate (a Japanese striking art), tae kwon do, and other styles.

Strikeforce athlete Marloes Coenen *(left)* punches Sarah Kaufman *(right)* during a 2010 match.

In the past, a fighter needed to know only one style of martial arts to be good at the sport. But that is not the case anymore. A fighter must be skilled in several styles to be successful. In fact, the different styles have blended together to form a unique MMA style of fighting.

Fighters mix their skills to make the most complete fighting style for them. For example, Silva uses Muay Thai, Brazilian jiujitsu, tae kwon do, judo, and capoeira (a Brazilian striking art). For Georges St-Pierre, the combination is karate and judo. MMA brings together an international mix of fighting styles. And it has a mix of stars from all over the world. The MMA fan base also spans the globe.

Georges St-Pierre (top) used his wide range of martial arts skills to win a UFC championship in 2008.

CHAPTER TWO

HISTORY AND CULTURE

MMA competitions have been around long before the UFC was created. Early forms of MMA include *pankration* from ancient Greece and *vale tudo* from Brazil.

Hercules (*left*) used pankration to defeat his enemies.

HEROES AND PANKRATION

ACCORDING TO ANCIENT GREEK LEGEND, FAMOUS WARRIORS HERCULES AND THESEUS INVENTED PANKRATION. BOTH BECAME EXPERTS IN THE MARTIAL ART.

Pankration competitions were held in ancient Greece.

Pankration is the oldest form of MMA. It dates back to at least the 600s B.C. In Greek, *pankration* means "all powers." It was the first no-holds-barred competition in recorded history. Pankration was used on the battlefield as a form of self-defense and in training as a sport. As a sport, pankration combined stand-up striking with wrestling, submissions (holds fighters cannot get out of), and strikes. Pankration became an event in the ancient Olympic Games in 648 B.C.

Vale tudo was developed in Brazil in the 1920s. These MMA contests were fought mostly in circuses and at informal gatherings. The no-holds-barred sport didn't become popular until the 1970s. The Gracie family, who created Brazilian jiujitsu, brought the contest to the United States. The Gracies were excellent vale tudo fighters. Vale tudo has become a popular sport worldwide.

Gerard Gordeau *(right)* took on sumo wrestler Teila Tuli *(left)* in UFC 1.

SUMO IN UFC

UFC 1 WAS TRULY A NO-HOLDS-BARRED COMPETITION. EVEN A SUMO WRESTLER, TEILA TULI, TOOK PART IN THE FIGHT. SUMO IS A JAPANESE FORM OF WRESTLING. TULI, WHO WEIGHED 415 POUNDS (188 KILOGRAMS), COMPETED AGAINST GERARD GORDEAU. BOTH MEN WERE OVER 6 FEET (1.8 METERS) TALL. BUT GORDEAU ONLY WEIGHED 216 POUNDS (98 KG). GORDEAU'S STYLE WAS SAVATE (FRENCH BOXING). HE WON WITH A KICK TO TULI'S FACE. THE LOSS KNOCKED TULI OUT OF THE REST OF THE COMPETITION.

THE UFC'S BEGINNINGS

MMA was popular in pockets of the world. But it didn't explode until the early 1990s, when Rorion Gracie created the UFC. Gracie's plan was to use the competition to find out which martial arts form was the best. The competition pitted top martial artists from many styles against one another in a no-rules competition.

Rorion is the son of Brazilian jiujitsu cofounder Helio Gracie. Rorion had opened a Brazilian jiujitsu school in California. He wanted to show the power of the family's style of fighting. His younger brother Royce entered the competition.

The first tournament, called UFC 1, was held in Denver, Colorado, in 1993. Eight fighters from several fight styles—including boxing, savate, and Brazilian jiujitsu—entered the tournament. Royce, the smallest competitor, won the tournament using Brazilian jiujitsu. His win helped spark interest in what would become the world's largest MMA organization.

Royce Gracie is lifted by his team after winning UFC 1.

TOP MMA SCHOOLS AROUND THE COUNTRY
- Grudge Training Center in Denver, Colorado
- Xtreme Couture in Las Vegas, Nevada
- American Kickboxing Academy in San Jose, California
- Jackson's Mixed Martial Arts in Albuquerque, New Mexico

MMA CULTURE

The UFC led to a cultural and martial arts revolution. A new wave of fight stars rose up. Pay-per-view fights bring in millions of dollars. The best fighters can earn hundreds of thousands of dollars for winning a single match. MMA schools have also sprouted up across the United States.

MOVIES, TELEVISION, AND VIDEO GAMES

Movies featuring MMA and MMA stars have made it to the big screen. They include *The Quest* (1996), a film about an MMA tournament. The film stars Jean-Claude Van Damme, an actor trained in Muay Thai. *Never Surrender* (2009) includes top UFC stars Georges St-Pierre, Anderson Silva, B. J. Penn, and Heath Herring. *Red Belt* (2008) includes UFC stars Randy Couture and John Machado. Randy Couture also joined actor Sylvester Stallone in the action-packed film *The Expendables* (2010).

John Machado (top) takes down an opponent in *Red Belt*.

Randy Couture (right) and Sylvester Stallone (center) played mercenaries in *The Expendables*.

13

The contestants on the first season of *The Ultimate Fighter* dramatically increased MMA's popularity in mainstream culture.

Among the most popular MMA cable TV shows is *The Ultimate Fighter*. This is a reality show that began in 2005. In it, fighters compete to win contracts in the UFC. Before this show aired, MMA could only be seen on pay-per-view. *The Ultimate Fighter* introduced MMA to more people. The series has started the careers of some of the biggest UFC stars. These include Forrest Griffin, Rashad Evans, Stephan Bonnar, Brendan Schaub, and Michael Bisping.

ACTION FIGURES AND CLOTHING LINES

MMA IS SO POPULAR THAT ITS STARS HAVE BECOME ACTION FIGURES. A BRAND CALLED ROUND 5 HAS MADE ACTION FIGURES OF COUTURE, ST-PIERRE, EVANS, AND CHUCK LIDDELL. MMA HAS ALSO INFLUENCED CLOTHING. BRANDS INCLUDE THE SUCCESSFUL TAPOUT, MMA OVERLOAD, AND REVGEAR.

Video fight games were popular before the UFC came along. With the UFC's growth, more video games feature MMA. EA Sports has MMA for PlayStation 3. UFC 2009 was designed for Xbox 360 and PlayStation 3. Both feature top MMA fighters as characters.

Forrest Griffin (left), who won the first season of The Ultimate Fighter, kicks Tito Ortiz (right) in UFC 106.

CHAPTER THREE

MOVES AND EQUIPMENT

One of the most recognizable fight rings in the world is the UFC's Octagon (an eight-sided box). Two competitors fight head to head in this 30-foot (9.1 m) diameter cage. The Octagon has a metal, chain-link fence around the edges.

Fighters need a lot of equipment for training. Athletes use mats, grappling gloves, and heavy bags for kicking and punching. They use focus mitts for practice hitting and pads for striking and kicking too. Fighters also use protective gear. The mouth guard is an important piece of protective equipment. Other protective gear includes shin guards, foot guards, and headgear. Different teachers require their students to wear different gear.

Hundreds of fans gathered around the Octagon to watch UFC 71 in Las Vegas, Nevada.

Germaine de Randamie (left) and Stephanie Webber (right) wear MMA grappling gloves during their 2011 match.

MMA grappling gloves are important. These are half-fingered gloves with padded knuckles. Their light weight and open fingers allow both striking and grappling moves. The gloves are worn in professional fights.

A huge part of being a good fighter comes down to strength and conditioning. The fighter must be skilled in fighting. But it is more important to be in top physical shape.

Taiwan's Zhang Jing Xiong (top) mounts his opponent, which puts him in excellent striking position.

18

STRIKING AND SUBMISSIONS

As students learn, they will find moves that they are naturally good at or simply prefer. Their height, weight, and strength determine much of this. Good body positioning is important in the sport. For some moves, fighters are able to stand up on the mat. Other moves work better on the ground. One key ground body position is the mount. In this position, a fighter straddles the opponent, who is lying on the ground. The two fighters are facing each other. This position allows a fighter to gain control of the opponent.

Women fighters attempt to gain control during a practice match.

UFC WEIGHT DIVISIONS

BANTAMWEIGHT: HAS A MAXIMUM WEIGHT OF **135** POUNDS (**61** KG)

FEATHERWEIGHT: HAS A MAXIMUM WEIGHT OF **145** POUNDS (**66** KG)

LIGHTWEIGHT: HAS A MAXIMUM WEIGHT OF **155** POUNDS (**70** KG)

WELTERWEIGHT: HAS A MAXIMUM WEIGHT OF **170** POUNDS (**77** KG)

MIDDLEWEIGHT: HAS A MAXIMUM WEIGHT OF **185** POUNDS (**84** KG)

LIGHT HEAVYWEIGHT: HAS A MAXIMUM WEIGHT OF **205** POUNDS (**93** KG)

HEAVYWEIGHT: HAS A MAXIMUM WEIGHT OF **265** POUNDS (**120** KG)

Striking moves include punches, kicks, and knee and elbow strikes. Punches are most often aimed at the opponent's head, but sometimes a punch can be effective to the torso. Kicks target the head, the legs, and the torso. Fighters most commonly use the roundhouse kick. It comes from karate and Muay Thai. The name comes from the circular motion the leg moves in. This kick targets the head, the body, and the legs. One of the best kickers and strikers in MMA is UFC middleweight champion Anderson Silva. He has knocked out 15 of his 32 opponents in his UFC career.

A submission is a finishing move that causes the opponent to tap out (give up) or the referee to stop the fight. A tap out occurs when a fighter taps the opponent or the mat during a submission.

Submissions are powerful moves. So fighters need to be careful while practicing them and using them in fights. Submissions include joint locks and chokes. Joint locks are when a joint is bent beyond its natural range of motion. Chokes slow the flow of oxygen or blood to the brain.

Top submission athletes include Antonio Rogerio Nogueira, a Brazilian jiujitsu black belt. His favorite move is the armlock, which bends the elbow a bit beyond its normal range. His favorite striking move is a hook to the stomach. Rashad Evans, former UFC light heavyweight champion, likes the Kimura, a type of armlock, as his favorite submission. His top strike is the left hook.

Diego Sanchez (right) fights Joe Stevenson (left) during a 2009 MMA match.

MORE MMA STARS AND FAVORITE MOVES

UFC FEATHERWEIGHT CHAMPION JOSE ALDO'S FAVORITE MOVE IS THE ARMLOCK. JAPANESE JUDO AND MMA FIGHTER YOSHIHIRO AKIYAMA'S FAVORITE MOVE INCLUDES ANY TYPE OF CHOKE. DIEGO SANCHEZ PREFERS THE REAR NAKED CHOKE, WHICH IS A CHOKE FROM THE BACK.

CHAPTER FOUR

COMPETITION

MMA has several levels of competitions as well as local and regional tournaments. Fighters compete at the lower levels early in their careers to get experience and attention. If they're good enough, MMA fighters move on to upper levels of competition. Besides UFC, these upper levels include Strikeforce and Bellator.

No high school, college, or Olympic-level MMA competitions exist. Rather, MMA is another career route for fighters who succeed in other martial arts. A tae kwon do or Muay Thai fighter might be very good. He or she may branch into MMA after picking up other fighting styles. For example, MMA star Brock Lesnar was a college wrestling star. And

EARNING THE CHAMPIONSHIP TITLE

THE LIST OF **UFC** CHAMPIONS CONSTANTLY CHANGES AS NEW CHALLENGERS DEFEAT CHAMPIONS. HOWEVER, WHEN A CHAMPION LOSES A FIGHT, HE OR SHE DOES NOT NECESSARILY LOSE THE TITLE. ONLY IF THE TITLE IS ON THE LINE CAN A NEW CHAMPION BE CROWNED.

Yushin Okami (right) punches Anderson Silva (left) during their middleweight title fight in 2011. Silva won the match.

Lyoto Machida began karate at the age of three and earned his black belt (a sign of the highest level of skill) as a teenager. He is a former UFC light heavyweight champion.

THE BASICS

MMA fight rules are very similar throughout levels and tournaments. The fights take place either in a metal cage or a boxing ring. Fighters wear the same clothes, usually shorts or long pants and no shirts. They also wear open-fingered gloves but do not wear shoes. A referee is in the ring, and three judges sit ringside. Up to five rounds are typically in a match.

A fighter wins by submission, knockout, technical knockout (when the referee decides the match cannot continue), stoppage because of injury, or a decision by the judges. A match can also end if a fighter's team gives up. This is called throwing in the towel. Sometimes a coach actually does toss a towel into the ring to signify defeat.

Judges' decisions are either unanimous (all judges agree) for one fighter or a split decision. This means one judge voted for one fighter and the other two for the winner. Judges score the fight on a 10-point system. The winner of each round gets 10 points. The loser gets nine points or fewer. The judges figure out how many points to give for each round. At the end of the match, the fighter with the most points is declared the winner.

A referee (right) steps in to stop the fighting during a match between Lyoto Machida (top) and Thiago Silva (bottom).

Illegal moves are aimed at preventing serious injury, although injuries still occur. A doctor makes sure Mark Hominick is okay after Hominick receives a blow to the head.

WHAT CAN'T BE DONE IN THE RING?

While the UFC at first had no rules, MMA competitions have become much safer. Several fighting moves have been made illegal. An illegal move, or foul, can result in loss of points or disqualification. Most fouls are actions that could severely injure a fighter.

Fouls include head butting, eye gouging, biting, hair pulling, and attacking the groin. Striking the throat, kicking or kneeing an opponent who is down, and stomping an opponent on the ground are also fouls. The referee calls the foul and may take points away from a fighter. A foul may injure a fighter so badly that the fighter cannot continue. The match can end in disqualification (if the foul was on purpose) or in no contest (if it was accidental). UFC middleweight champion Anderson Silva lost one fight by a foul. He kicked Yushin Okami while Okami was on the mat.

Top female competitor Cris Santos *(left)* punches her opponent during a Strikeforce match.

FEMALE FIGHTERS

UFC president Dana White has banned women from competition. But they do compete in Strikeforce. Each match has three three-minute rounds. Cris Santos is one of the top fighter's in women's MMA. She has a background in Brazilian jiujitsu. Santos won the first Strikeforce middleweight championship in 2009.

INTERNATIONAL AND REGIONAL COMPETITIONS

MMA competitions are held around the globe. For example, major 2011 fights were held in Toronto, Canada; Rio de Janeiro, Brazil; and Las Vegas, Nevada.

Hundreds of smaller, regional fights take place across the United States each year. These aren't as widely watched as professional MMA fights. Athletes fight in smaller matches first. If they win a number of fights, they start to get noticed at higher levels.

MMA is the hottest thing on the worldwide fight scene. Television, movies, books, games, and clothing are all part of this martial arts explosion. It has also boosted individual styles of martial arts around the world.

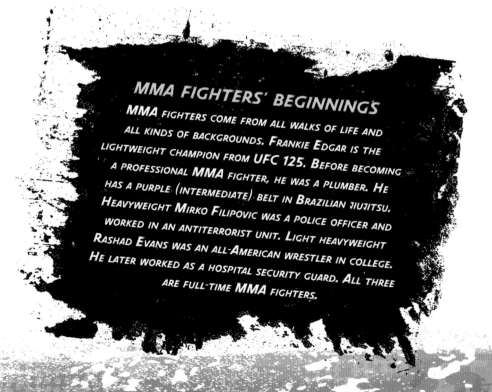

MMA FIGHTERS' BEGINNINGS

MMA FIGHTERS COME FROM ALL WALKS OF LIFE AND ALL KINDS OF BACKGROUNDS. FRANKIE EDGAR IS THE LIGHTWEIGHT CHAMPION FROM UFC 125. BEFORE BECOMING A PROFESSIONAL MMA FIGHTER, HE WAS A PLUMBER. HE HAS A PURPLE (INTERMEDIATE) BELT IN BRAZILIAN JIUJITSU. HEAVYWEIGHT MIRKO FILIPOVIC WAS A POLICE OFFICER AND WORKED IN AN ANTITERRORIST UNIT. LIGHT HEAVYWEIGHT RASHAD EVANS WAS AN ALL-AMERICAN WRESTLER IN COLLEGE. HE LATER WORKED AS A HOSPITAL SECURITY GUARD. ALL THREE ARE FULL-TIME MMA FIGHTERS.

POPULAR MOVES

REAR NAKED CHOKE

FOR THIS MOVE, A FIGHTER STARTS BEHIND THE OPPONENT ON THE MAT. THE FIGHTER CIRCLES THE LEGS BEHIND THE OPPONENT'S MIDSECTION. THEN THE FIGHTER MOVES ONE ARM AROUND THE OPPONENT'S NECK AND GRABS THAT ARM WITH THE OTHER ARM. THIS FORMS A TIGHT LOCK AROUND THE OPPONENT'S NECK.

ELBOW

A FIGHTER DRIVES THE BACK LEG INTO THE FLOOR AND STANDS TALL. THE FIGHTER BENDS THE ARM AND SWINGS THE POINT OF THE ELBOW INTO THE OPPONENT. THE ELBOW CAN BE SWUNG UP, DOWN, OR ACROSS THE FIGHTER'S BODY.

A rear naked choke

ARMLOCK

A FIGHTER STARTS AT THE SIDE OF THE OPPONENT. THE FIGHTER GRABS ON TO THE OPPONENT'S ARM AND SCISSORS THE LEGS AROUND IT. THE FIGHTER'S KNEES ARE SLIGHTLY BENT. ONCE IN THIS POSITION, THE FIGHTER PULLS THE OPPONENT'S FIST TOWARD THE FIGHTER'S CHIN, STRAIGHTENING THE ARM.

An armlock

2011 UFC CHAMPIONS

BANTAMWEIGHT:
Dominick Cruz

FEATHERWEIGHT:
Jose Aldo

LIGHTWEIGHT:
Frankie Edgar

WELTERWEIGHT:
Georges St-Pierre

MIDDLEWEIGHT:
Anderson Silva

LIGHT HEAVYWEIGHT:
Jon Jones

HEAVYWEIGHT:
Cain Velasquez

Cain Velasquez

HALL OF FAME

The first man inducted into the UFC Hall of Fame was Royce Gracie in 2003. Gracie won the first UFC tournament and is one of the best Brazilian jiujitsu fighters in the world. Other fighters inducted include Ken Shamrock, Dan Severn, Randy Couture, Mark Coleman, Chuck Liddell, and Matt Hughes.

29

GLOSSARY

COMBAT

an active fight between groups or individuals

CONDITIONING

the process of training to get in good physical shape

MERCENARY

a hired soldier who serves for wages only

NO-HOLDS-BARRED

free of rules and restrictions

PAY-PER-VIEW

cable TV that viewers can order for a fee

REFEREE

a person who judges or guides a sporting event

REVOLUTION

a sudden change

TORSO

the midsection of the human body

UNANIMOUS

having the agreement of all

FOR MORE INFORMATION

FURTHER READING

Gogerly, Liz. *Capoeira: Fusing Dance and Martial Arts.* Minneapolis: Lerner Publications Company, 2012.

Wells, Garrison. *Amateur Wrestling: Combat on the Mat.* Minneapolis: Lerner Publications Company, 2012.

Wells, Garrison. *Brazilian Jiujitsu: Ground-Fighting Combat.* Minneapolis: Lerner Publications Company, 2012.

WEBSITES

MMA Fighting

http://www.mmafighting.com

This website features MMA news as well as stats and videos of top athletes in Bellator, Strikeforce, and the UFC.

Strikeforce

http://www.strikeforce.com

The official website of Strikeforce includes information on top fighters, upcoming events, and tickets.

Ultimate Fighting Championship

http://www.ufc.com

The official website of the Ultimate Fighting Championship includes information on all fighters in the organization and upcoming events. Visitors can also post in forums and play MMA-related games.

INDEX

ABOUT THE AUTHOR

Garrison Wells is a third-degree black belt in Nihon jujitsu, a first-degree black belt in judo, a third-degree black belt in Goju-ryu karate, and a first-degree black belt in kobudo. He is also an award-winning journalist and writer. Wells lives in Colorado.